THE RAINFOREST BOOK

DK

DISCOVER THE WORLD'S
TROPICAL RAINFORESTS

Tropical rainforests cover less than 3 percent of the planet, yet they contain at least half of all the world's wildlife. This makes them fascinating and important places.

Let's travel through these enchanting tropical worlds by discovering the huge variety of plants and animals that live there.

WHERE DO YOU FIND RAINFORESTS?

The **EQUATOR** is an imaginary line that runs around the middle of the Earth like a belt. **TROPICAL RAINFORESTS** are found in places near the Equator, where it is warm year-round, and wet for most of the year.

Above and below the Equator, the temperature is cooler, but you can still find rainforests growing in areas where there is a lot of rain. These rainforests are called **TEMPERATE RAINFORESTS.**

TROPICAL RAINFORESTS:

TEMPERATE RAINFORESTS:

THE EQUATOR ⟶

The area between the yellow lines is called the **TROPICAL ZONE.**

The **Amazon** is the largest tropical rainforest and has one of the world's longest rivers running through it.

A tropical rainforest will get at least 79 in (2 m) of rain every year. But sometimes, this amount can be more than 394 in (10 m). The temperature is normally 72–93°F (22–34°C).

THERE ARE DIFFERENT TYPES OF TROPICAL RAINFORESTS.

Some tropical forests are called **cloud forests**. They grow on mountains and hills among damp, low clouds.

Tropical forests growing near the sea are called **mangrove forests**. Here mangrove trees grow with their roots sunk deep into the salty water.

Most tropical rainforests grow in low areas of land where rivers flow. These are the rainforests that most people think of when they hear the word "**jungle**."

HOW DO PLANTS AND ANIMALS LIVE?

An enormous variety of plants and animals live in tropical rainforests. All these living things need food to give them energy to survive, but plants and animals get their food in different ways.

PLANTS ARE ABLE TO MAKE THEIR OWN FOOD.

A plant's leaves act like food factories. They make the food using three things:

 LIGHT from the sun

 CARBON DIOXIDE from the air

 **WATER** from the ground

While plants are making food, they release **OXYGEN** into the air. This is a gas that all animals need to breathe.

.......The **flowers** make **seeds,** which can grow into new plants.

On some plants, the seeds are found in fruits.

The **stem** .... carries water to the leaves.

The **leaves** absorb energy from the sun to help make food. ....

Melastome plant

The **roots** take ..... up water and nutrients from the soil.

In every rainforest there are thousands of different types of plants, which provide food and shelter for animals.

6

ANIMALS GET THEIR FOOD FROM EATING OTHER LIVING THINGS.

Iguana

An **HERBIVORE** is an animal that eats only plants.

Bat

A **FRUGIVORE** is an animal that mainly eats fruits.

A **NECTIVORE** is an animal that mainly eats nectar, a sweet liquid made by the flowers of plants.

Hummingbird

An **INSECTIVORE** is an animal that mainly eats insects.

Anteater

Toucan

An **OMNIVORE** is an animal that eats both plants and other animals.

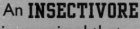

Jaguar

A **CARNIVORE** is an animal that mainly eats other animals.

In a rainforest, animals and plants need each other to survive. One way that plants and animals are connected is through **FOOD CHAINS**.

Seeds and berries get eaten by the bird.

The bird gets eaten by the snake.

The snake is eaten by the eagle.

WHAT DOES A RAINFOREST LOOK LIKE?

Tropical rainforests such as the Amazon contain some of the world's tallest trees. At the very top, the sun shines brightly onto their leaves. But as we travel down toward the rainforest floor, it gets darker because more tree leaves, branches, and other plants block out the sunlight.

Some animals that live in the emergent layer will never set foot on the forest floor, but they may travel to the understory to find food.

EMERGENT LAYER: At the top of the trees there is little shelter from the wind and rain. But some monkeys like to hang out here, swinging between the branches.

CANOPY: More wildlife lives here than in all the other layers. In the canopy there are thick tree branches, leaves dappled with sunlight, and a refreshing breeze.

UNDERSTORY: Leafy bushes and small trees make up this dark and hot area, where frogs hide and birds find food.

FOREST FLOOR: Covered in fallen leaves, the dark and damp forest floor is the perfect habitat for insects, as well as insect-eating animals such as anteaters.

The clouds release rainwater back into the forest.

The water in the air rises and forms clouds.

WHY ARE RAINFORESTS SO WET?

The air in a rainforest feels wet and sticky because trees and plants release water that they don't need. This moisture rises when it is heated by the sun. High up in the air, the moisture forms clouds that release rainwater back into the rainforest below.

Plants release water into the air.

THE RIVER: Streams and rivers flow through lowland rainforests. In these waters we find alligatorlike reptiles called caimans, and fish such as piranhas.

WHY ARE RAINFORESTS IMPORTANT?

RAINFORESTS GIVE US FOOD.

More than 3,000 types of fruit can be found in rainforests, including wild versions of bananas, oranges, and mangoes. Even a favorite treat, chocolate, comes from cacao trees that grow in rainforests.

RAINFORESTS CREATE RAINWATER.

The moisture released into the air by rainforest plants and trees rises up to form clouds. These clouds can travel to places that would otherwise be very dry, where they release rainwater.

RAINFORESTS STOP FLOODS.

Tree roots suck up rainwater. Without trees, water could wash the soil away into rivers and block them, which would cause flooding.

RAINFORESTS CREATE THE AIR WE BREATHE.

Rainforests are known as the lungs of the planet because their plants create oxygen that all animals, including humans, need to breathe.

RAINFORESTS ABSORB CARBON DIOXIDE.

Carbon dioxide is a gas that animals breathe out. It is also created by burning fossil fuels, such as oil and coal, which we use to make electricity and power cars. Having too much carbon dioxide in the air causes extreme changes to the weather and harms the environment. The rainforest is full of plants that help protect the environment by absorbing carbon dioxide from the air.

RAINFORESTS GIVE US MEDICINE.

Around a quarter of the ingredients found in medicines come from rainforest plants. For example, tropical cinchona trees produce quinine, which helps treat malaria.

MILLIONS OF PEOPLE LIVE IN RAINFORESTS.

These people have expert knowledge of rainforest plants and animals, and use the nature around them to make their shelters, food, and medicines.

RAINFORESTS ARE HOME TO AN ENORMOUS NUMBER OF THE WORLD'S PLANTS AND ANIMALS...

DISCOVER AN **AMAZING** VARIETY OF RAINFOREST **PLANTS**

Rainforests are lush, green worlds filled with thousands of plant species, from towering trees tangled with vines, to feathery ferns sprouting on every branch. But while rainforests might sound like natural paradises, most plants there must compete with each other to survive.

Let's learn about the unique ways that tropical plants find sunlight and reproduce.

In the Amazon, up to 400 different species of trees can exist in just one hectare of land—an area similar to the size of a soccer field.

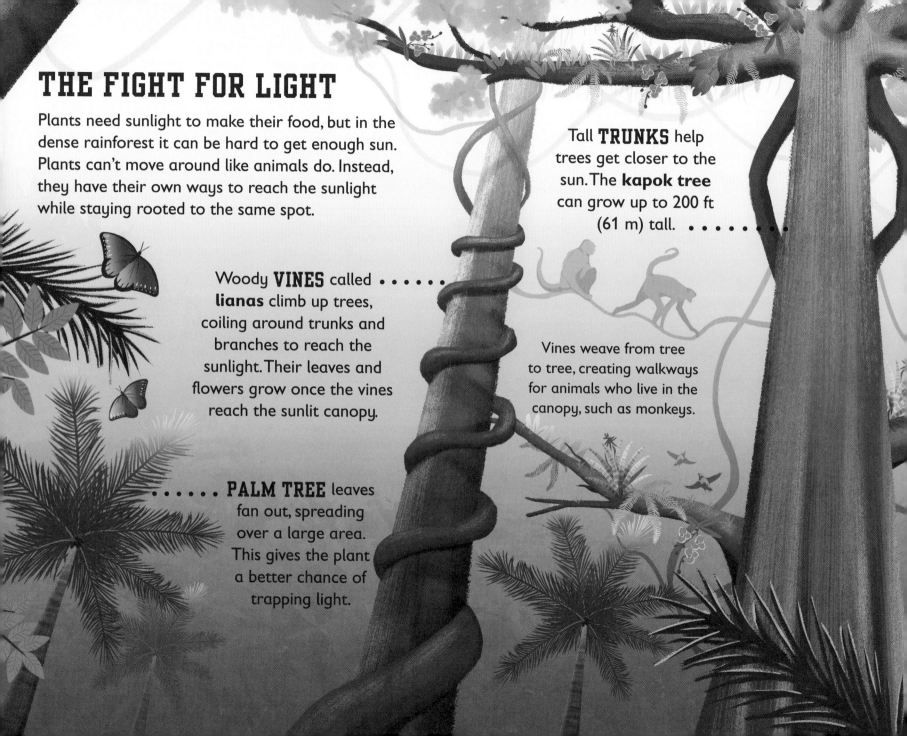

THE FIGHT FOR LIGHT

Plants need sunlight to make their food, but in the dense rainforest it can be hard to get enough sun. Plants can't move around like animals do. Instead, they have their own ways to reach the sunlight while staying rooted to the same spot.

Tall **TRUNKS** help trees get closer to the sun. The **kapok tree** can grow up to 200 ft (61 m) tall. . . . .

Woody **VINES** called . . . . . . **lianas** climb up trees, coiling around trunks and branches to reach the sunlight. Their leaves and flowers grow once the vines reach the sunlit canopy.

Vines weave from tree to tree, creating walkways for animals who live in the canopy, such as monkeys.

. . . . . . **PALM TREE** leaves fan out, spreading over a large area. This gives the plant a better chance of trapping light.

Small plants called **EPIPHYTES** don't grow from the forest floor, but live high up on tree branches where there is more light. They live off soil and water that gets carried by the wind, so they are also known as air plants.

Bromeliad plants live high up on branches. Their leaves collect rainwater in pools, creating little watery habitats for tree frogs.

Birds that live in the canopy stop at bromeliads for a drink.

Instead of growing up toward the sun, a **strangler fig** starts life at the top of another tree. Its roots grow toward the ground, spiraling down the tree's trunk until they reach the forest floor.

Eventually, the tree inside is surrounded by winding roots and can't get any light. The tree dies, and the strangler fig takes its place.

PLANTS AND THEIR POLLINATORS

While some plants have thorns and poisonous leaves to stop animals from eating them, other plants do what they can to attract particular animals called **POLLINATORS**. Pollinators visit plants and move pollen from flower to flower. This important job is called **POLLINATION** and plants need it to grow seeds.

HOW DO ANIMALS POLLINATE FLOWERS?

1.
A pollinator, such as this **orchid bee**, looks out for flowers, which provide food from among their petals. This food is **nectar**.

2.
While drinking the nectar, pollen gets stuck to its face or body.

3.
When the pollinator goes to the next flower, the pollen rubs off its body onto the flower.

A bee's tongue is called a **proboscis**. It is very long so that it can reach into flowers for nectar.

4.
After pollen has been moved from one flower to another, the plant grows a **seed**. This will eventually grow into a whole new plant.

Brazil nut tree flowers

The orange powder is **pollen**.

Pollen comes off a part of the flower called the **stamen**.

MEET THE POLLINATORS

Flowers come in many shapes, sizes, colors, and smells. Different variations attract different kinds of pollinators.

COLORFUL FLOWERS attract

insects and birds that look for nectar in the day.

The **hermit hummingbird** has a long, curved beak that reaches into **heliconia flowers**. ....

.........The female **orchid bee** pollinates **Brazil nut tree flowers**. Pollinators of this plant must be strong enough to push open the flowers' tightly closed petals to reach the nectar.

Some butterflies love to visit the **monkey brush vine**, as it has lots of stamens. The stamens brush pollen onto visitors.

WHITE FLOWERS

stand out in the dark to attract nocturnal pollinators such as bats.

BIGGER FLOWERS are

visited by larger pollinators such as mammals and birds. The **kinkajou** is a nocturnal mammal that pollinates **balsa tree flowers**.

PLANTS AND THEIR SEED SPREADERS

Once a plant has been pollinated, its seeds grow. Plants need their seeds to be spread far and wide, so they pack them into tasty, colorful fruits that animals will want to eat.

SUPER SEEDS

During or after eating the fruit, animals drop the seeds on the ground, where they can grow into new plants. But for the seeds to grow, they need to be strong and sturdy so that they don't get damaged by the fall.

Some seeds are **POISONOUS**, so when animals such as monkeys and bats eat the fleshy fruit, they drop the toxic seeds to the ground.

The **cashew fruit** has two parts—a sweet, juicy cashew apple fruit and a toxic seed hanging below it. ....

Seeds that are too **BIG** and hard for animals to eat get dropped to the ground.

Spider monkeys eat the fleshy fruit around a big **mango** seed. ....

..........Toucans eat **nutmeg** seeds whole. Each seed has a soft outer coating that the bird digests, but it coughs up the hard, poisonous inner seed.

Some seeds have a **HARD CASING** to protect them.

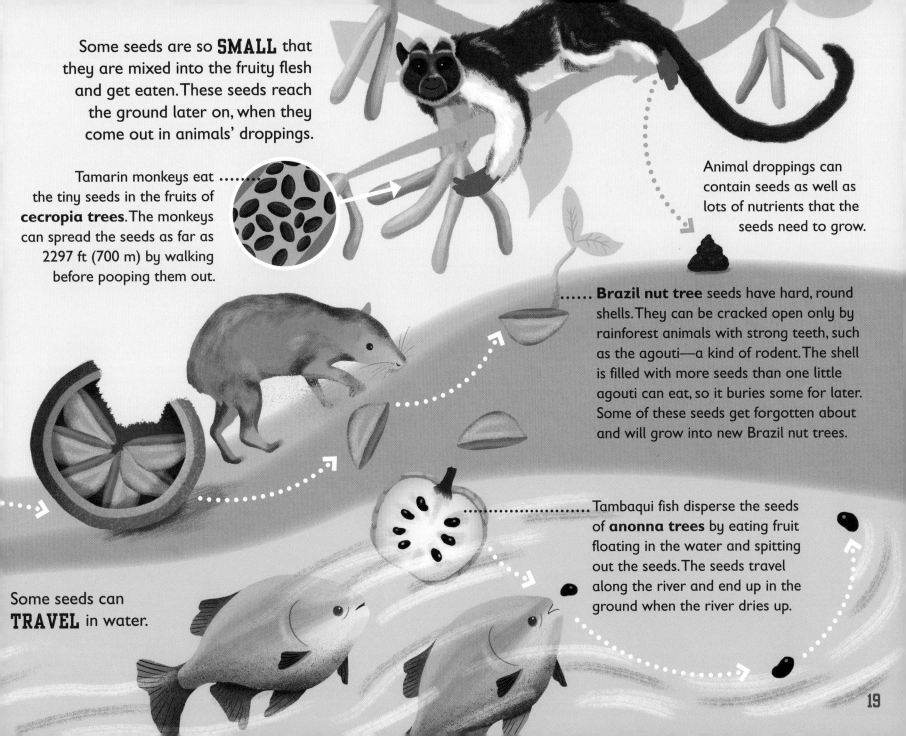

Some seeds are so **SMALL** that they are mixed into the fruity flesh and get eaten. These seeds reach the ground later on, when they come out in animals' droppings.

Tamarin monkeys eat the tiny seeds in the fruits of **cecropia trees**. The monkeys can spread the seeds as far as 2297 ft (700 m) by walking before pooping them out.

Animal droppings can contain seeds as well as lots of nutrients that the seeds need to grow.

Brazil nut tree seeds have hard, round shells. They can be cracked open only by rainforest animals with strong teeth, such as the agouti—a kind of rodent. The shell is filled with more seeds than one little agouti can eat, so it buries some for later. Some of these seeds get forgotten about and will grow into new Brazil nut trees.

Some seeds can **TRAVEL** in water.

Tambaqui fish disperse the seeds of **anonna trees** by eating fruit floating in the water and spitting out the seeds. The seeds travel along the river and end up in the ground when the river dries up.

19

THE CYCLE OF LIFE

Fallen seeds sprout on the forest floor and new life begins. But the forest floor is also the place where life ends, as dead trees and leaves fall to the ground. This is all part of an important cycle. The rotting bark and leaves return nutrients to the soil, which new plants need to grow.

HIDDEN HABITATS

On the forest floor, dead leaves and branches make a **LITTER LAYER** above the soil. This warm, dark layer provides food and homes for many small creatures.

Harvestmen are harmless relatives of spiders that eat rotting plants.

Termites are wood-eating insects. They live in huge colonies and build nests out of chewed wood in trees or under the ground.

Dung beetles roll animal poop into balls. They use it later as food for their babies, called larvae, which hatch from their eggs.

Glow worms dig themselves into the mud, leaving just their luminous (shining) heads sticking out, ready to bite any creature that walks past.

Maggots

Velvet worms are slow-moving predators that squirt a sticky glue to trap insects.

BREAKING IT DOWN

Many creatures that make their homes here are known as **DECOMPOSERS**. They eat dead leaves and plants, breaking them down into smaller parts that go into the soil as nutrients.

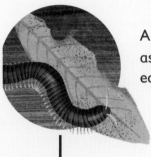

A decomposer, such as this **millipede**, eats a rotting leaf.

The leaf breaks down into smaller parts in the millipede's gut and is pooped out.

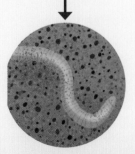

In the soil, other decomposers, such as **earthworms**, break down the leaf even more. The small parts become nutrients for plants.

Fallen trees leave gaps in the rainforest canopy, allowing sunlight to shine onto the forest floor. This light gives seedlings the energy they need to sprout, and new trees, known as pioneer trees, start to grow.

FUNGI such as mushrooms and toadstools live on dead matter. They recycle rotting plants, turning them into nutrients in the soil.

Plant roots absorb nutrients from the soil.

21

MEET THE WONDERFUL ANIMALS THAT LIVE IN TROPICAL RAINFORESTS

There is an incredible variety of animals to be found in tropical rainforests. In these dense forests, where predators lurk around every corner, each animal faces the challenge of finding food while staying safe.

Let's take a look at the amazing ways that rainforest animals survive, and discover what makes every creature unique.

There are more species of animals in the rainforest than in any other habitat in the world. For example, while the entire continent of Europe has a mere 53 species of frogs, the rainforests of Peru and Ecuador contain more than 300 frog species.

ANIMAL HUNTERS

Day and night, the animals of the Amazon face the challenge of finding food. For carnivores and omnivores, the next meal is often on the move and difficult to find. Animal predators need sharp senses, lightning-fast reactions, and cunning strategies to capture their prey.

A SMART SPIDER

Unlike other spiders, a **jumping spider** doesn't build a sticky web. Instead, it makes a plan of attack. Using its excellent vision, the spider plans a route to creep up on its prey. When it gets close, the spider launches itself onto the unlucky insect, jumping lengths of up to 50 times its own body size.

A CUNNING CLIMBER

Between tree branches, a **green vine snake** stretches its pencil-thin body to silently hover over prey such as lizards. While the lizard is unaware of the danger dangling above, the snake strikes, lifting it off the branch and killing it with its venom.

A PATIENT POUNCER

The large **Surinam horned frog** sits and waits in the mud and leaves on the forest floor. When its prey wanders within reach, the frog springs out and swallows it whole. The frog is nicknamed "Pac-Man frog" for its huge mouth and amazing appetite for insects, mice, and frogs.

A HAIRY HUNTER

Tarantulas can't see much in the dark, so instead, they use touch to hunt. Special hairs on their legs detect the vibrations of moving bugs and small animals such as lizards and bats. From the vibrations, the tarantula can tell the exact size and location of its prey. Then it attacks, injecting its prey with deadly venom from its fangs.

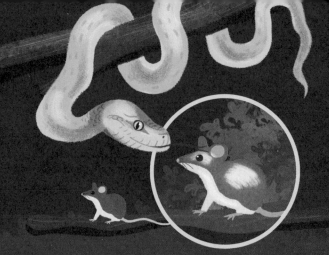

A SIXTH SENSE

Scent and vision are important senses for snakes, but **pit viper snakes** have an extra sense that they use to catch prey: they can "see" heat. Special organs between their nostrils and eyes detect the body heat of prey such as mice, bats, and birds. This gives the snake a picture of the size and location of the animal when it is dark.

A CAMOUFLAGED CAT

Whether it is day or night, the spotted fur of a **jaguar** keeps it hidden in the bushes as it stalks its prey. Padded paws allow it to move silently until it pounces, sinking its sharp teeth into its prey. Unlike other cats, jaguars don't mind water, and sometimes hunt for fish, turtles, or caimans in the river.

A DEADLY DRIFTER

A **black caiman** is one of the largest predators in the Amazon rainforest. Its eyes and nostrils are at the top of its head, so it can see and breathe while most of its body remains hidden underwater. The caiman mostly hunts at night and drifts slowly toward its prey before striking.

CAMOUFLAGING CREATURES

Some rainforest animals have evolved to become experts at hiding from predators. Many animals have colours and patterns to blend in with their surroundings—a trait called camouflage.

The underside of a **blue morpho butterfly**'s wings are a dull brown so that it is hidden against tree bark when it is resting.

But the top of its wings are a dazzling blue, so it flashes from brown to blue as its wings open and close. This creates an effect that looks like flickering sunlight and confuses predators.

Just as the leaves on a tree all look slightly different, **katydid** insects come in various shades of green, and some even look like dead or half-eaten leaves.

A **leaf-tailed gecko** has a frilled edge on its skin that lies flat against tree bark. This disguises the gecko's shape, making it harder for predators to spot.

Malayan horned frogs hide among dead leaves.

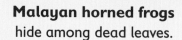

Stick insect

COLORFUL WARNINGS

These animals aren't shy of predators. Their bright colors and patterns make them stand out and act as a warning that they should not be eaten.

Heliconius butterflies lay their eggs on the leaves of poisonous **passion flower vines**.

The eggs hatch into caterpillars that are able to eat the leaves.

Eating these leaves means that the caterpillars develop into butterflies with the plant's toxic chemicals in their bodies.

Predators such as birds avoid eating heliconius butterflies because they recognize their markings and know that the butterflies are toxic.

Coral snakes have bright red and yellow stripes to warn predators of their potent venom.

Stink bug

The bright colors and patterns of **poison dart frogs** warn predators of their deadly defenses. Their skin is coated in poison. The frogs make this poison from chemicals in the insects that they eat.

MEET THE MIMICS

Not all colorful creatures are poisonous. These frogs, butterflies, and snakes have similar colors and patterns to their poisonous lookalikes, so that they too can have the same dangerous reputation in the rainforest.

Heliconius-mimicking moth

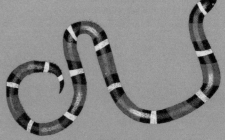

Milk snake

Zaparo's poison frog

27

SAFETY IN NUMBERS

Some animals stay safe in the rainforest by living in large groups. Sticking together when there are predators around, and while building homes and finding food, can help them survive.

THE HOME BUILDERS

Green tree ants are impressive insect architects. The colony works as a group to make their nest. Some ants pull leaves together so that others can bind them using their larvae's silk.

Larvae are carried in the ant's jaws. They produce a sticky silk that glues leaves together.

While building, ants hold onto each other to make bridges for other ants to cross. Their home can take hours to build, but once it is complete, it will be a safe place for larvae to grow into adult ants.

THE FOOD FORAGERS

Howler monkeys live in a group called a troop. Each morning, the troop howls together to warn other monkeys to stay away from the trees that they feed on.

A howler monkey troop contains about 6 to 15 monkeys.

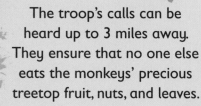

The troop's calls can be heard up to 3 miles away. They ensure that no one else eats the monkeys' precious treetop fruit, nuts, and leaves.

The otters work together to defend their home by swimming toward a predator and barking loudly at it.

LOOKING OUT FOR EACH OTHER

Giant river otters live in family groups and sleep, play, travel, and feed together. They make dens by burrowing into the side of the Amazon River. They are protective of their home—the whole family looks out for danger, alerting one another with snorting sounds if a caiman is approaching.

FOLLOWING THE LEADER

In a **gorilla** troop, the oldest and strongest of the male gorillas is the leader, called the silverback. He keeps the group safe by leading them to food, deciding when they will sleep, and protecting them from danger.

Mountain gorillas can be found roaming the tropical cloud forests of central Africa. They live in troops of up to 30, which usually contain several young males, some females, and lots of young gorillas.

29

FINDING A MATE

Although many animals try to stay safely out of sight in the rainforest, it sometimes pays off to stand out from the crowd—especially when it comes to finding a mate.

PUTTING ON A SHOW

For animals that are awake during the day, looks can be important. Some birds of paradise found in New Guinea, a large tropical island north of Australia, have evolved to have impressive feathers and funky dances to attract a female.

Female western parotia

The male **western parotia** clears the ground of sticks and leaves to create his dance floor. He then takes a bow before performing a whirling dance.

AN IMPRESSIVE BUILDER

The male **Vogelkop bowerbird** impresses his date by building a giant structure out of twigs, which he carpets with fluffy moss. The structure, called a bower, is large enough for a human to crawl inside and can take years to make.

Female Vogelkop bowerbird

The bowerbird collects flowers, berries, and fungi. He neatly arranges his treasure into different colored piles around the bower.

A SHOW OF STRENGTH

The male **rhinoceros beetle** has huge horns, which it uses as a weapon to go into battle with other males. Each beetle can lift more than 100 times their own body weight. The winner of the fight will drive the other beetle away, clearing its territory of any competition and successfully attracting a female beetle.

THE LOUDEST CROAK

Being colorful is not so impressive when it is dark. For nocturnal animals, having a loud voice is a much better way to be admired. At night, a rainforest comes alive with the different croaks and calls that are unique to each frog species.

Warty rainforest frog

Many male frogs have flexible skin around their throats that expands like a balloon when they croak. This helps make their calls louder.

New Guinea bush frog

Female frogs listen out for the unique call of their own species. Some females like the sound of deep croaks, while others find long, complex calls more desirable.

31

GROWING UP IN THE RAINFOREST

With poisonous plants and deadly predators around every corner, growing up in the rainforest is challenging. While some animals are born equipped with everything they need to survive, others have a lot to learn from their parents.

Durian fruit

ORANGUTANS are some of the most devoted mothers in the Sumatran rainforest. They spend eight years looking after their young, teaching them all that they need to know.

Baby orangutans watch their moms carefully. This way, they learn how to gather around 400 different kinds of food, remembering which trees grow fruit and when.

Mothers show the young orangutans how to build a nest with folded branches.

A tricky skill to learn is how to use tools. For example, twigs can be used to pick termites out of their woody nests.

SUN BEARS are the world's smallest bears. Females give birth to one or two babies, called cubs. Cubs stay close to their mothers for two years, learning how to climb trees and find food.

RHINOCEROS HORNBILL BIRDS make their nests inside the tree holes left by sun bears. After mothers have laid their eggs inside a hole, they build a muddy wall to keep predators away.

Sun bears can poke their long tongues into bees' nests to find honey, their favorite food.

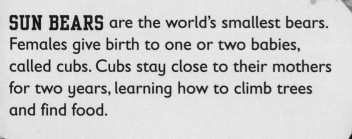

Sun bears use their long claws to rip holes into bark to find termites to eat.

Hornbill mothers stay sealed inside trees for around three months, keeping their eggs warm and caring for the chicks after they hatch. When the chicks are old enough to leave the nest, their parents chip away at the muddy wall to let them out.

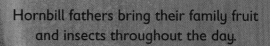

Hornbill fathers bring their family fruit and insects throughout the day.

33

WHY DO RAINFORESTS NEED PROTECTION?

Sadly, rainforest animals face even bigger challenges than their daily struggle to find food and raise a family. Around the world, their rainforest homes are under threat, with trees being chopped down at an alarming rate.

Let's understand why this is happening and what can be done to help the rainforests.

Trees store carbon, which can be harmful to the environment. It is released into the atmosphere when trees are cut down. One rainforest tree can contain 3–4 metric tons of carbon—around the same amount that a car emits over four years.

DEFORESTATION

Rainforest trees provide habitats for amazing animals and are important to the health of the planet. However, all over the world, these trees are being cut down to use the land beneath them. This is called **DEFORESTATION**.

WHY ARE RAINFORESTS BEING CUT DOWN?

Many trees are cut down so the wood can be used to make furniture and paper. This is called **LOGGING**.

People clear rainforest land to build **ROADS** and **CITIES**.

People cut down rainforest trees to make space for **FARMS** and **RANCHES**, where we grow crops and raise cattle for beef.

Rainforest trees can be cut down to make space to plant oil palm trees. The fruits from these trees are collected for their **PALM OIL**, which is in lots of things we eat or use, including chocolate, shampoo, and soap.

WHY IS DEFORESTATION BAD?

HABITAT DESTRUCTION

Rainforest trees are habitats for lots of animals. Just a single tree can be home to more than 150 beetle species. When trees are cut down, animals are left with nowhere to live.

CLIMATE CHANGE

Trees absorb and store carbon dioxide—a gas that can be harmful to the environment. When there are fewer trees, more carbon dioxide stays in the air. Carbon dioxide traps heat from the sun, so when there is lots of it in the atmosphere, the Earth gets hotter. This causes problems such as extreme weather.

LOSS OF BIODIVERSITY

If there are fewer trees and plants, it is harder for animals to find the food they need to survive. And without animals around to help, there are fewer ways for plants and trees to disperse their seeds.

FLOODING

When trees are cut down, it leaves open areas of land. In these spaces, rainwater collects and runs into rivers, which can overflow and cause flooding.

HOW DOES CLIMATE CHANGE AFFECT RAINFORESTS?

For tropical rainforests, climate change means hotter weather and less rain. When there is unusually dry weather for a long time, it is called a **DROUGHT**. Droughts cause many problems for animals and people living in rainforests, as well as for the rest of the world.

When there is less rainfall, it is difficult for plants to grow. This affects local farmers who grow crops such as coffee, bananas, lemons, and peanuts to make money and feed their families.

A bad crop season in the rainforest affects people all over the world, too. It means that foods grown in the rainforest, such as corn, wheat, soybeans, and rice, will be in short supply.

If the weather gets hotter, trees in the rainforest will produce fruit at unusual times of year. This confuses the animals that rely on the fruits for food.

When there are fewer trees, climate change gets worse. Less carbon dioxide gets absorbed, so there is more in the air.

There are a lot of people working to protect rainforests from fires. NASA has a satellite system that collects information to predict when forest fires might happen. This means that action can be taken to stop them from spreading.

Animals cannot adapt as quickly as humans when the world they live in changes. When the temperature increases and there is less rain, it can disrupt their entire life cycle.

When it is hot and dry, destructive forest fires are much more likely to happen. Fires can blaze over a huge area, burning trees and killing wildlife.

When it is dry, the rainforest cannot recover as quickly from the damage that has been done, and it is likely that fires will occur again.

RAINFOREST RECOVERY

There are lots of people in the world who are protecting rainforests and the amazing plants and animals that live there. These people are called **CONSERVATIONISTS**.

PROTECTED AREAS

Conservationists can work with governments and local communities to make rules that protect areas of rainforest from logging and farming. In these areas, they study plants and animals and look after endangered species so that their numbers can increase.

REFORESTATION

One important way to protect wildlife and fight climate change is to plant trees. When lots of trees are planted in areas of cleared rainforest, it is called reforestation. This helps improve the health of the soil, provide homes for animals, and reduce the amount of carbon dioxide in the air.

SUSTAINABLE FARMING

Farming is an important part of rainforest life. It helps feed local communities, as well as providing fruits, nuts, and oils for people across the world. However, farming can destroy plants and animals and harm the world's climate.

Conservationists are trying to change the way that people farm in rainforests. New ways of farming can help the farmers as well as supporting rainforest plants and animals.

Farming uses up important nutrients in soil, so when crops have grown, farmers have to move on and clear new areas of land to use. Composting is a way of recycling plant waste to put nutrients back into soil, so farmers can use the same area of land over again.

Planting a mixture of crops prevents weeds from growing. This means that harmful weed-killing chemicals don't need to be used on the land.

Seed banks are also a great way to protect plants. A seed bank stores precious seeds, which can later be planted to keep certain crops from dying out.

Planting some native species of plants—species that are naturally found in rainforests—will support wildlife and attract pollinating insects.

41

HOW CAN YOU HELP?

FIND OUT MORE

To find out more about rainforests, you can read books, watch documentaries, and visit rainforest conservation websites. Then you can share the facts with your friends and family! The more people understand how precious rainforests are, the more people will protect them.

LOOK BEFORE YOU BUY

If you are buying paper or something made of wood, look for the FSC logo. FSC-certified products have been made with less harm to rainforests.

SUPPORT CONSERVATION GROUPS

There are lots of fun ways to help people who work to protect tropical wildlife. You could raise money with your school, family, or friends by having a bake sale or a sponsored run.

RECYCLE PAPER

When paper is recycled, it can be reused, or made into more paper. This means that fewer trees have to be cut down to make paper.

REDUCE YOUR CARBON FOOTPRINT

Reducing your carbon footprint means reducing the amount of carbon dioxide you put into the air, as this is harmful to the environment. You can do this by choosing to walk or cycle instead of driving when you can, and by using less electricity in your home.

PLANT A TREE

Planting a tree in your garden or with your school will help fight climate change because trees make oxygen and absorb carbon dioxide from the air.

EAT LESS MEAT

This can help reduce your carbon footprint. Fewer cattle herds would be needed, so fewer rainforests would be cut down to make space for them to graze.

LOOK OUT FOR PALM OIL

It's hard to avoid buying palm oil when it's in so many of the things we eat and use. But you can look for products that have been made with sustainably sourced palm oil. This comes from oil palm trees that have been grown in a way that doesn't harm rainforests as much.

MAKE YOUR OWN MINI RAINFOREST

Learning how plants and animals survive teaches scientists how to protect them. You can study tropical plants like a scientist by making a **TERRARIUM.** A terrarium provides a warm and humid place for tropical plants to grow—your very own miniature rainforest!

TO MAKE A TERRARIUM YOU WILL NEED:

A large glass container with a lid, such as a cookie jar, or you could reuse a large pickle jar.

Small rocks or pebbles—you can collect these from outside.

Activated charcoal to keep the soil healthy.

Potting soil to grow the plants in.

You will be able to find the plants, soil, and charcoal at a garden center.

1–3 small tropical plants, such as palms and ferns.

5.

Lightly spray water onto the plants and place the lid on top. Put the jar in a well-lit spot.

4.

Plant your tropical plants by placing them in the wells in the soil.

3.

Water the soil if it feels dry and make some small wells for your plants.

2.

Next, add a layer of activated charcoal, followed by a thick layer of soil.

1.

At the bottom of the jar, add a 1-inch (2.5-cm) layer of small rocks.

Open the lid once every couple of weeks to give the plants some fresh air.

THE WATER CYCLE

You can see the rainforest water cycle for yourself in your terrarium. You will notice water droplets on the inside of the jar, where the plants have released moisture. These droplets will drip back down into the soil, where the plants will absorb the water through their roots, starting the cycle again.

You could decorate your terrarium with some small toys or models of rainforest creatures. Which animals might you see in a tropical rainforest?

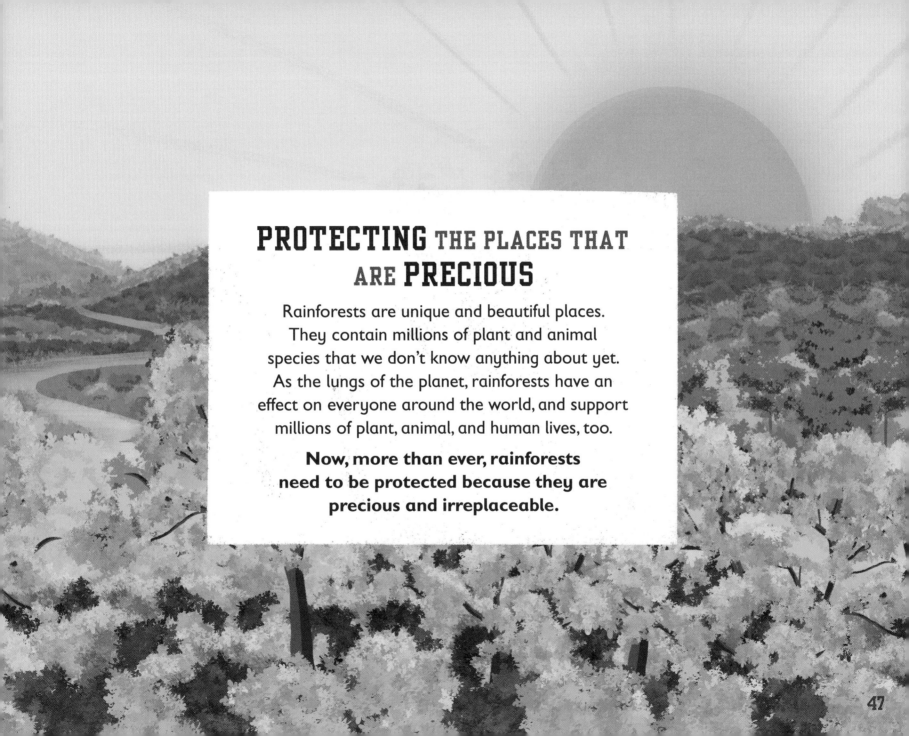

PROTECTING THE PLACES THAT ARE PRECIOUS

Rainforests are unique and beautiful places. They contain millions of plant and animal species that we don't know anything about yet. As the lungs of the planet, rainforests have an effect on everyone around the world, and support millions of plant, animal, and human lives, too.

Now, more than ever, rainforests need to be protected because they are precious and irreplaceable.

WILDLIFE INDEX

Author and Illustrator Charlotte Milner
Editor Sophie Parkes
US Executive Editor Lori Hand
Editorial Assistant Becky Walsh
Managing Editor Penny Smith
Managing Art Editor Mabel Chan
Art Director Helen Senior
Publishing Director Sarah Larter
Production Editor Abi Maxwell
Production Controller Basia Ossowska
Consultant Dr. Andrew Whitworth

First American Edition, 2021
Published in the United States by DK Publishing
1450 Broadway, Suite 801, New York, NY 10018
Text and illustration copyright © 2021 Charlotte Milner
Design copyright © 2021 Dorling Kindersley Limited
DK, a Division of Penguin Random House LLC
21 22 23 24 25 10 9 8 7 6 5 4 3 2 1
001–315386–Feb/2021

Published in Great Britain by
Dorling Kindersley Limited
A catalog record for this book
is available from the Library of Congress.
ISBN 978-0-7440-2663-4
DK books are available at special discounts when purchased in bulk for sales promotions, premiums, fund-raising, or educational use. For details, contact:
DK Publishing Special Markets, 1450 Broadway, Suite 801, New York, NY 10018 SpecialSales@dk.com

Printed and bound in China

For the curious
www.dk.com

ABOUT THE AUTHOR

Charlotte Milner creates books with playful designs to bring important information to young readers. Her books explore environmental conservation issues and inspire a love of the natural world.